hemispheres
inside a stroke

karen lazar

hemispheres
inside a stroke

modjaji books

Publication © Modjaji Books 2011
Text © Karen Lazar 2011
First published in 2011 by Modjaji Books PTY Ltd
P O Box 385, Athlone, 7760, South Africa
modjaji.books@gmail.com
http://modjaji.book.co.za
www.modjajibooks.co.za

ISBN 978-1-920397-24-1

Book and cover design by Natascha Mostert
Edited by Nella Freund
Printed and bound by Mega Digital, Cape Town
Set in Garamond

For Claire, Raphael
and Julia

Contents

The Journey of the Writing

THIS BOOK TRACKS the three phases of a journey so far: firstly, 'Acute Metamorphosis', then 'Rehabilitation', and then 'Adaptation'. Each of these phases contains elements of the others and none is yet complete.

The genre of this story emerged intuitively, of its own accord. My stroke initially brought with it many spatial, perceptual and subjective changes, which worked against my apprehending the condition with a single 360-degree view. Rather, I could only grasp the stroke in facets, and cumulatively, over time. My perceptions wrote themselves as short prose fragments rather than as a continuous narrative. Whilst most of the shifts in perception and spatial field have corrected themselves over the decade since the stroke, I have still sought to capture, from the inside, a faceted representation that honours an experience bigger than the sum of its parts.

Some of the pieces are vignettes of the memorable people I have met along the way. Many of them, with fewer resources than me, have taught me a grace, courage, humour and stoicism I never imagined possible in the face of such challenges. This volume is for you.

The Beginning

I WAKE UP on an ordinary morning in early February feeling well. It's clear and sunny. After twenty years of teaching English at university, I've moved to a new job, corporate but educational. I've been there five days.

I have an important strategic planning meeting today with senior members of the team. Since I'm the new girl, I'm nervous but excited.

I dress extra carefully. I put eyeliner on in my mirror, closing one eye to do the other, as usual. But a strange thing happens. A murky grey-black wash covers over the mirror and for a moment I can't see myself. I try again but it's still there. I abandon the make-up and drive myself to the office, aware that my left eye is doing all the work.

During the meeting certain people disappear depending on the angle of my head, like characters departing stage-right. I start to feel frightened but I reason that maybe my glasses need updating or that I'm a bit stressed. At lunchtime I phone my ophthalmologist of many years. She tells me to come in for a check immediately.

She runs through the usual tests, conversing normally. There's a photo of her twin girls and her boy on the desk. I feel reassured by them.

Then she does a light check with a tiny bright torch. She zooms in. She shines the torch directly into my right eye. I'm looking at her fine-boned face, blue eyes and a tendril of russet hair.

Her face tightens unmistakeably into a look of alarm.

"I need to send you for some more tests. Your optic nerve is not responding to light," she says. "There are a couple of explanations. This could be an eye infection, an unusual migraine, or something else. I don't know what's going on, but I'm sending you to an excellent colleague for a brain scan."

I arrange for someone to do the school-lift. My children are nine and six years old.

Late that afternoon, I cross the road from the Rosebank Clinic's X-ray department to the neurologist, holding my MRI results in a sealed envelope. It's surprisingly heavy. I'm disoriented from the examination and the radiologist's injection of contrast medium into my vein with a syringe big enough for an ox.

The traffic on my right side is invisible so I sidle across the road like a crab, using my left eye. Having one black field makes the light brighter on the good eye. I feel nauseous from the glare.

The neurologist calls me in. He barely looks at me, and doesn't use my name. I sit opposite him at the desk. He takes the pictures out of the envelope and puts them on the viewing box. He scans the report.

I look at half a sunset through his window.

He gets up and gruffly calls my mother from the waiting room.

Before she sits down, we both know the answer.

"There's a large mass pressing down on Karen's right optic nerve. The radiologist suggests it's a meningioma – a benign tumour – but we don't know for sure."

It's been surreptitiously growing for a long time. There have been few warning signs.

My mother squeezes my hand, softly. She's outwardly calm. The tears I've been holding back all day surge up in both the seeing and the obstructed eye.

We carefully discuss a plan of action. We'll see a brain surgeon and take it from there.

And so begins the traipse from doctor to doctor, the numb repetition of the story, the bright lights, the needles, the waiting, the worry. We go into a flurry of incredulous research and data finding.

We decide to go for surgical removal of the tumour, soon, lest it cross the mid-line and blind the left eye too. More than anything, I want to see my children grow up and I want to be able to read the written words that are my livelihood.

On balance, the possible benefits of the operation seem to outweigh the risks of leaving the tumour in my head. My small daughter calls it The Tuna.

All the family members brace themselves. My three apprehensive siblings plan back-to-back visits from London and California.

The day comes. The hospital is ghostly quiet. It takes a while for us to realise why. It's March 21, a public holiday – Human Rights Day – previously the anniversary of a massacre. There's an irony at work but I'm too numb with terror to figure out what it is.

The operation is nine hours long. The tumour has put out tendrils, yet it is successfully removed in its entirety, and it is not malignant. The eye is saved. This is the desired outcome; a brilliant feat of surgery.

But the brain is a sensitive and irritable organ and does not like a scalpel poking around in it for so many hours. After my scalp has been stapled together from ear to ear, a crucial blood vessel in the brain either collapses or clots. We will never know, but the nett result is the same. The normal oxygen flow to a portion of my brain has been denied; a large area of the motor cortex, which governs movement, has been irreversibly damaged. In the early days the effects are inconclusive. We wait.

Strokes vary in kind, severity and location in the brain. A stroke on one hemisphere of the brain crosses over to manifest in possible paralysis, or hemiplegia, on the opposite side of the body. Language, cognition and sensation may undergo changes, depending on the type of stroke the person has had. My stroke occurred on the right hemisphere of the brain, leaving the left side of my body affected but speech and language intact.

In the ICU period I'm grappling, or not yet succeeding in grappling, with a double metamorphosis. To start with, there's the challenge of having had my cranium cut open.

Nobody can remain the same after that. Then there are the repercussions – this strange new creature called a stroke, through whose lens the world has changed beyond the words to say it. I cannot find the syntax to put 'my' and 'stroke' in the same sentence for a long time.

But I can see. Mainly medical machines and doctors and nurses, but perfectly nonetheless. I can see the velvety texture and pollen grains on the flame-coloured flowers a friend brings me. I can see my family's brave, caring faces. My visual world is back, more vivid and more whole than ever.

I'm not allowed to see my children for a month, though. My head is bandaged over its shorn strip; my face is black with bruising, and contorted to the left. But I'm told the children are surrounded by loving people and doing as well as can be expected. Their father bears their shock and his own changes with extraordinary strength.

I start to think about the private losses. One of the hardest is that I will not dance again.

But there's a story to be told, and if I can't dance, at least I can write.

Cluster One
Acute Metamorphosis

The Corridor

THE CORRIDOR SEEMS endless. From the entrance at the top, it slopes down towards the various ICUs – merciless titles evoking lives saved and ceded.

I am wheeled up from Neuro-ICU several dozen times during the first two months; I become well-acquainted with the corridor, its semi-circular apses every few metres, in which families huddle while waiting for news from the operating theatres. Gauguin-like pictures line the walls of the corridor, horribly colourful and tropical. The mood is surreal.

Sometimes we are three abreast in our metal beds, heads turning to ascertain the spectrum of adjacent frailties. Meal trolleys exuding moist cabbage weave round the transport of fresh laundry to the wards. Staff mouth news at each other. This corridor probably conveys five hundred people a day. The air is ancient.

In the ward, tired Matron picks up the telephone, "Porter for Lazar to Radiology, please." I wonder what millimetre of change in my brain the camera will yield today, and what stem-cell research will yield in my lifetime.

We regulars have gotten to know some of the porters by name and sight. Today, Simphiwe pushes me up the corridor. He is young and fresh-faced and encouraging.

"You look better today." He prides himself on being able to turn a bed round a corner with snug perfection. "You see, I got my licence."

Simphiwe leaves me with an extra blanket in the humbler corridor of the X-ray department. The radiographers smile at the mundane task of positioning a kneecap jostled in football. For scarier organs they work quietly in pairs.

In idle moments I get flashbacks of the original journey up the corridor. Quarter to six in the morning, heading for brain surgery. Too late to change the decision. My jetlagged brother John walks along with me to the very threshold of the theatre, until he can't come any further. We both know what doesn't need to be said.

"Bye Karrie."

In theatre they're playing the radio, Bob Marley's *Buffalo Soldier*. I'm astonished to find myself singing the chorus before I sink into oblivion.

The Recovery Room

THIS INBETWEEN ROOM belongs in an earlier phase of evolution when we had gills. The space swims. My consciousness bobs like flotsam and jetsam. It is too bright and too dark at the same time. At last two adored faces float into view: my brother and mother. They, at least, are human, but I wonder why I haven't seen them for a century and why they're holding on to each other.

The atmosphere changes like a coup d'état. Figures run around me. The machines attached to me throb and vibrate. The new entity – the pain that is to become my permanent visitor – introduces itself with a slam.

The earliest voice of my life, from another liquid place, says, "Karrie, move your left side."

I trust this voice, so I try.

But I can't move, I can only surrender to the deep, wondering why this windowless tank is called the recovery room.

Morphine

I'M MESMERISED BY watching the steady drip-drip of the liquid into my vein.

My perceptions are muffled but amplified. Is that the morphine or the stroke? I'm a newcomer to both.

Oh, the exquisite release from pain.

Sometimes my mind ducks and dives, though to others I insist it doesn't. One lunchtime, a platter of glistening boerewors and pap appears before me – ethnic food, they call it. We order our meals by ticking a card each day. But I cannot eat this and wouldn't have ordered it. It's too big, too greasy, too wrong. The error unnerves me.

"I didn't order this, sorry. Where's my sister?"

My sister Gillian steps round the curtain, carrying the reality principle with a smile. I feel like she's thrown me a lifeline.

" Here I am. You did order it, darling. Let's see if someone else wants it and get you some fruit."

But at night the hallucinations are graver than a meal misordered. I descend fathoms away from my known self and see sinister figures in ICU refusing to give me help or bringing messages I don't get.

Even the day's waking nightmare is better than this drugged, dislocated consciousness that delivers the unconscious out of its basement where it belongs.

Denzil

WHEN MY NEIGHBOUR asks Denzil if he ever wanted to study medicine, he says, "What makes you think I didn't study medicine? Nursing covers anatomy, pharmacology, psychology."

He's a male nurse, fifty-something, with a smooth brown face and tight curls. He is witty, mischievous, but not inappropriate. He keeps photos of his grandchildren in his pocket.

Denzil loves his vocation, has no qualms about being in a female profession. He pours a male strength into a soft touch. He cackles about his secondary status as ward handyman, on call to crank up beds and fix bells. He's the only nurse on the ward to treat the doctors politely, but not reverentially.

He has a framework for our interaction. On the first day he notices me stiffen as he washes me in the bath. He reads my face.

"Listen, this is only awkward for me if it's awkward for you. I'm a professional. This is what I do."

He believes in light and air, opening curtains and windows as soon as he arrives. Seeing our ward looks on to a concrete wall, he moves a vase of flowers on to the windowsill, and stands back to admire his work.

"There, that's better feng shooey."

He's the first person I see in the morning, a welcome shape bearing tea; he sets the tone for the day. His habit, as he leaves at night, is to remind us of what we've accomplished during the day- two extra steps, a meal well eaten, a visit from colleagues.

The patients' favourite part of the day is the changing of the guard at night. The black nurses cluster at the exit of the ward to sing hymns, soothing themselves and us in beautiful *a capella* after an arduous day.

Denzil weaves his own soft baritone line around the women's voices.

Mind-Matter

I SLIDE ON an electric bed deep into the sputnik. This is not for claustrophobes. The CAT scan, a miracle of modern technology that can reach to where the ordinary human eye and hand cannot. Bone, flesh, muscle, tumour are made as visible as film.

I'm very cold, though wedges are packed tightly around me so that no part of me can move. Sputnik prefers cold and stasis. The scan begins with a quick spinning noise; decisive regular cuts recording the picture.

The radiographers are in the adjacent space, looking through a window into the scan room, and typing instructions into their computers. They are white-coated and pony-tailed and alert, both the men and the women. How did I get into *Bladerunner*?

My mother sits, quiet and watchful, protected from harmful rays by a lead apron too big for her strong little form. We know the drill, she and I; we've done this before.

From inside the machine I have a small view of a monitor mounted on the wall opposite. On the screen appears the age-old image: the walnut of the human brain, folds and hemispheres and stem. The picture is beautiful in a subtle, astral way.

Hang on, that's *my* brain. How is it possible to be thinking these thoughts and looking at my brain at the same time?

The technicians are warming to their task. They tap their keyboards to get a low-angle shot of my brain, swivelling airily in virtual space. Odd, because it feels so tightly packed in here.

Is that my mind I'm looking at? Is that consciousness, 14cm by 10cm, poised for the camera, with its flanks exposed?

Or is it mere matter?

Cross Words

NEUROLOGICAL ICU, FOUR-THIRTY in the morning. It's pitch dark except for a chilly blue light at the nurses' station. I'm watching a few of them on break sipping coffee and doing crossword puzzles. I marvel that they are still alert after working such a long night.

"Number six across – 'band around the middle'– that would be E-Q-U-A-T-O-R," says a middle-aged nurse with a stern haircut and a polka-dotted mug. "Here's a tough one," she goes on. "Number nine down, intersecting my last word: 'Told by witches that his descendants will be kings.' O dear, someone help me, I'm stuck!"

"Banquo," I murmur, very relieved that my cognition hasn't disappeared along with my mobility. I try out a few other random ideas in my head to see whether I'm still myself. I seem to be.

I'm aware that my ward neighbour, the man who fell three storeys off a scaffold without a helmet, hasn't made a sound for hours. I wonder if he's dead. I'd heard them say he was close. A nurse bustles out of his cubicle with an air of normalcy; I breathe a sigh of relief. Polka-dot rustles her newspaper and chews her pencil in irritation at the clue.

My other neighbour, known only as 'the young head injury' because no one has shown an interest in his name, is thrashing his gauzy head around and loudly calling for a cigarette. Matron bounds forth, bosoms first, holding a peeved sign: 'There Will Be No Smoking In This ICU'.

"Anyway, it's five in the morning, Doctor would never allow it."

I wonder if she is as horrible to her children, as triumphant in their failures, as she is to her patients.

A few days later I hear that the boy has sprung out of semi-coma and been seen chain-smoking in the corridor outside ICU. I like him. But right now I wish he would shut up so I can go back to sleep before the brain surgeon's brisk morning visit.

I fret that the nurses will forget to help me brush my teeth before I have to contemplate the surgeon's impeccable ones.

Yellow Jersey

I DECIDE TO start small, by opening the fingers on my left hand. I give pure concentration to this small act. Nothing happens. The arm and hand are immovable, fingers tightly curled into a ball. I try to wriggle my left toes. I pull the sheet off so I can see them. Again nothing happens. There they are, pink and still, mine but not-mine. The message isn't coming through from brain to extremities. Telecommunication is down.

So this is what it's like now.

In week two of the stroke, a sport-loving friend gets a message through to me in ICU. I'm wafting in and out of consciousness but the message is welcome.

It says, "Karen, the road ahead is going to be like a hundred Tours de France in endurance and staying-power. But we all think you can do it."

It makes me think about human endeavour, the will to conquer the odds. I read my message again, warmed by the faith and motivation my friend has tried to impart. I think of the great cycle race he got me interested in, in another life. A momentary picture of myself bed-bound in the bright yellow jersey comes to mind. But I'm still in the aseptic green hospital gown. Maybe I should get some yellow pyjamas. This place is too dark anyway.

Previously in my life, if I tried hard enough, the effort invariably resulted in what I wanted. Hubris, or tenacity? I was always talentless in maths, but sheer stubborn slog got me good results. Yet, here I am, in a body where some endeavours will only ever yield an alien failure. Can I tap into that reservoir of stubbornness now?

I'm not so drugged that I can't register the metaphysical benefits of a softer definition of conquest.

Cluster Two

Rehabilitation

Airwaves

DECADES AGO, SPECIALLY segregated hospitals were built for the men with ravaged lungs who came up from the catacombs of wealth upon which the city burgeoned.

These days the 'disease profile' has changed, and so too must the business of medicine. Rehabilitation now includes those damaged by the mad roads and lifestyles above the ground's surface.

And so we inhabit different wings of the same hospital. Occasionally we peer out at each other's quarters. The mining ward has windows grim and cloudy from overcrowding and wheezing.

One day an offsides man lumbers into our ward. He could be forty or seventy, and his face is blue-black from struggle. His breath is ragged.

"Hello, I'm Themba," he says, pulling up a chair next to my neighbour who is sharing his fruit basket with the other patients.

Themba hacks and coughs for several minutes. Matron Sheila brings him a swathe of paper towel from the washbasin, and a blue plastic mask with elastic to go behind the ears.

"Eh, you cover your face in my ward; TB flies like water in a fountain."

"Sorry ma'am," says Themba, anxiously, to me. I'm in my steel bed, reading a paper and half-listening.

"I got this very bad sickness of the airwaves," he says.

"Airways," retorts Sheila from her station.

Nowadays the hospital has to share a hill with an equally vast neighbour, the ungainly National Broadcasting Corporation. It alternates cement with blue glass; huge satellite dishes spinning in the draughts. Its buildings squeeze us into odder and odder recovery rooms, held up by vertiginous stilts. 'When space runs out, build over or under' says the hospital's manifesto of architectural survival.

At the apex of our hill stands the Brixton broadcasting tower, pointy as a minaret and visible for miles.

Themba has pushed his mask aside and is busy eating a pear, watched by an alert Sheila. As matron, her chief responsibility is Infection Control. Though stroke and spinal damage aren't contagious to others, our collective immunity is low.

"You're going in one minute," she says to Themba.

There are four television sets in our ward, placed close together in a span. The patients and nurses mainly watch news and football and soapies. A small arena of chairs and wheelchairs blocks the floor space.

More often the quadruple screens are not watched at all, but remain ceaselessly on, white noise and flicker buzzing at our membranes. At night I burrow under the sheets for blankness, until Sister Eunace the night matron eventually decides to switch off all four sets and warm her hands on her tea.

The quality of the TV picture is the ward's dominant obsession, after food. Sheila's elegant height mandates her to twiddle the dials by day.

It does seem inexplicable that our picture is so bad, when it's being beamed from three hundred meters away.

"I'm gonna watch the match at four tomorrow," says Themba, weakly getting up to go. "See you then."

"I suppose he'll want tea," clicks Sheila.

Wanda

THE MORNING IS grey with carnage and cold porridge. Those of us who are dressed and can sit up are wheeled to the tables. First there is Stroke table, weak and asymmetrical; even I, the youngest by thirty years. Then Gunshot table, heads lolling and weals livid. Lastly Truck Accident table, lovely young men remembering the two days without sleep, and the moment of downhill knowledge towards an object that didn't vanish.

We survey each other, interested in the metal and stitches and apparatuses that hold one another together, human carapaces made external. Some try to smile and compare erratic doctors.

Zaid, a beautiful young boy, is going home today. He declines breakfast.

"Going home today," some of us intone. Picturing our own distant homes and declining thoughts of how we will manage.

Back at Stroke table, the patients are being comradely. "I've got two working hands, let me cut up your sausage." The nurse serving breakfast puts milk in my tea without asking. I don't drink milky tea but I've been waiting for a hot drink for six hours, and I cannot bring myself to complain within this hierarchy of hungers. Nausea and anxiety flood me. My neighbour at the table puts his hand on my cup. "I'll drink it, I could use a second cup." He adds four spoons of sugar to it.

Wanda breezes in, pushing an incongruous turquoise wheelchair. Wandile Ebenezer Tunzi. He is a porter and he is miraculous. He is lithe and strong and stylish and could be in a gym, a habitat of beautiful bodies. We all adore him. For he has come to take us down to Physiotherapy, one by one, to start the effort of daily bodily hope.

"Lazar, you're first today," he twinkles at me. I cheer up immediately. Work, that's something I know how to do. I am sped down the corridor, tea-less but safe. In the close metal lift, with doors that open onto hospital smells on each side, Wanda tells me he would like to train to be a physiotherapist himself.

Once in the Rehab Room, Wanda settles me on to an exercise plinth and brings me a tiny glass of guava juice, on my working side so I can reach it.

"Solly next, Wanda," says a physiotherapist, half the age of the patient so named.

"Oh, you mean Mr Masilu," returns Wanda, not skipping a beat.

I watch another stroke patient from my ward, a pretty woman with an absent look, stride up and down the therapy bars and tie her own shoelaces. How does she get to be so lucky?

"Minor stroke," says Wanda, "and she's been here eighteen months."

Mr Masilu is having a mutinous day. He sits on his plinth, his body bulky, limbs disassociated, unmanned.

I sweat, and ponder the exodus of my command.

The Physio room is getting busy. Local radio blares to no listeners. Wanda is in all four corners at once, answering the phones, mopping up urine, untrussing suspended patients.

"Wandile, take Mr Masilu to Occupational Therapy," commands the head physio. But Mr M has one thought alone for his survival today: back to bed. He and Wanda exchange vernaculars, and I notice they do not wheel out of the door towards Occupational Therapy.

It is not yet nine o'clock.

Keeping Occupied

IN THE VAST Rehab Clinic with its freezing corridors, the least hospitable room is Occupational Therapy. It is dark and low ceilinged and dungeon-like.

Here we, the brain-changed, are at our most vulnerable. Is it that our new incapacity is most brought home to us there?

Wanda and Jacinto, the indomitable porters, work together in creative traffic control.

We queue in our wheelchairs, suspicious and irritable, for a desk to become available for each of us. Then we are given tasks to bring us back to our functioning selves. We wriggle into sweaters, we do story sums, we scour telephone directories for places we will never reach, so that our skills can be evaluated. The therapists rally and make notes.

Some of us cry with frustration, or cheat by peering at the neighbouring desk.

I'm given a jigsaw puzzle, with Donald and Daisy Duck in eternal colourful inanity, courting each other. One of the trainee therapists says, "She's got a PhD, shouldn't she have something more sophisticated?"

"No," bridles the head of OT, sapped by her own authority. "She's been affected like everyone else."

She's right. I line up the flat edges and the corners of the scuffed pieces, but the ducks will not come together.

Later I'm moved to the simulated kitchen. It has been donated by an annual Kitchenex exhibition, and it's glossy and lovely. All surfaces are at wheelchair level and there are clever nooks and crannies for stowing. It's the closest most of the patients will ever get to a kitchen that isn't a mere kettle, a gas cylinder and a tin mug and plate.

We have been instructed to make muffins, four women with five working limbs between us. We hold the mixing bowls between our legs. There's a dusty fall-out, but eventually our fragrant achievement is borne out proudly back into the dungeon.

There's not enough to go around.

.

Fractions

SATURDAY MORNING IN the Rehab Clinic. Our usual physiotherapist is off for the day and an unfamiliar one called Lynne comes in to work with us. She looks harassed. She's in her middle years and exudes both experience and attrition. She quickly assesses each of us and does the core exercises. That means maintaining the muscles that still work and trying to strengthen those that are wasted. We roll and twist and reach and bridge. It's basic, but we tire easily.

We're all listless and bleak that the weekends are no different from the weeks. We watch Lynne warily, as eager to be finished as she is.

Lynne reads my card and goes through a physical appraisal with flinty eyes. Whilst flexing and stretching my paralysed limbs, she says,

"It must have been very hard for you coming round from your op feeling like half a person."

I'm too stunned to talk back. The physio moves on to my neighbour who gives me a wan thumbs-up signal.

Only years later, do I realise Lynne triggered in me a fiery embracing of a new truth:

I have never been more whole.

Doctors

"DOCTORS COMING," CALLS the sentinel from the corridor. Figures scurry to stuff fallen blankets back into cupboards, to pluck dead flowers from their vases. A trail of face-washing down the rows spruces up the patients for our first performance of the day.

We feel like a crowd of naughty locals awaiting a Raj Inspector.

Enter Dr Fabrizio. His first patient is Mrs Kekana, an elderly diabetic who has been admitted for aggravating stroke.

"Why you so fat?" he snaps, poking a patch of flesh under the ragged nightie. "I'm gonna have to wire your jaws together for the rest of your life."

I seethe from the bed opposite.

"Lazarrre," his tongue rolls as he passes my bed. We are mutually relieved not to be assigned to one another.

"Bowel movement yet?" Dr Fabrizio quizzes his next baffled patient. "Why not?"

Dr Mouton, a young, graceful doctor, has started his rounds. He dares to repair, where he can.

"Don't worry, Mama," he says to Mrs Kekana. "We're not going to wire up your mouth. You're not feeling well, have a rest."

Chief medical man, Dr Ferguson, is now on the ward. No one knows how he got to be so senior, other than through longevity and habit. He looks like Winnie the Pooh, and clutches a worn medical bag akimbo on his chest, but never opens it. We all entertain ourselves with his idiosyncrasies. He likes to make patients drink a saline enema for a variety of unrelated and inverted maladies.

"How are we today?" he asks me jovially.

I ignore the plural. He calls a female nurse to uncover my body.

"Still paralysed?"

"No shit, Einstein," under my breath.

The youngest nurse looks abashed when Dr Ferguson points out that my neighbour's blood pressure has not been taken. She squeezes past the bear tummy to do it.

"Tell the family to come and remove him on Friday; he's been here long enough. I need the bed," Dr Fabrizio resounds further down the ward, swinging his stethoscope for a miniature unseen Tarzan.

Dr Watson is poised at the threshold of the ward. Her first name is something feminine and literary, Vanessa or Virginia, and she invites us to use it. She sizes up the chaos, and takes a back route to her first patient.

She and Dr Mouton confer about a problem. Dr Ferguson abstractedly fingers a greasy thermometer in a cup.

As if by secret signal, the doctors are gone. The ward breaks into a babble.

The nurses gather swiftly at their station to co-decipher the doctors' hasty notes.

Mrs Kekana's grandson, Jabu, opens two sachets of artificial sweetener onto her cereal, and grimaces to himself at the taste. He feeds her lovingly.

The next tier of healers will be here soon. Overstretched social workers and tolerant speech and swallowing trainers. We brace ourselves for the day's multifarious endeavours.

The doctors will come back tonight, aloof and exhausted.

Night-thing

I AM ONE of those who cannot abide the ragged scuttle of any night-thing across the floor.

After midnight, I am sleepless and isolated in the grey lozenge of my curtained bed.

"There's a rat on the ward," I hear one nurse cheerfully tell another. I tumble over the precipice of panic, and strain my gaze to the floor to see if I can see it. My eyes go up a level to the forty metal curtain rails surrounding forty innocent beds. Rails surely born to be carriageways to snouts and tails going somewhere on a dark mission.

I am close to tears. I try reasoning.

"This is a hospital, you are safe from vermin here." Civilisation created hospitals to defy them. Didn't it? But I can't reassure myself. I turn to wondering whether I would even feel it if the thing ran over me, since I still feel nothing else on my skin, at least on the left side. Could paralysis have so gloriously happy a benefit? I tuck my sheets into a tight angry cocoon, alert to primeval threat.

Should I be feeling compassion for all God's creatures, maybe? I decide against it. This ward full of broken people summonses more tenderness than I have surfeit for. I hope somebody assassinates this night-beast, and soon.

Next day, I tell my friend, mocking myself to her smiling, head-shaking gaze. But I see the flicker of 'anything's possible in this place' cross her face. Years later she tells me she saw a rodent as big as a shoebox confidently marauding around the kitchen when she went to fetch my fruit salad from the fridge.

But she does not tell me then.

Pig

Two ELDERLY MEN felled by stroke are brought into the ward one week. The first is in a fury of injustice, writhing against his condition.

"Jesus Christ! Jesus Christ."

This is not supplication, this is rage.

"Jesus fucking Christ." His wife winces. Her thin fingers go up to her throat, as if to reassure the small gold cross that she is not implicated in this ugliness.

"Please Donald, be quiet. You can't bully Jesus, you need to speak to him quietly, then he will help you. Please stop swearing, you're upsetting the other patients."

"Bugger them. Jesus Christ."

It doesn't stop, except during meals. It reaches a crescendo at night, when the solitude of sleeping among forty strangers in an alien body hits him. I simply cannot slough off either he or his maligned deity, because my bed is back-to-back with his, heads almost touching. I feel like a captive pushmi-pullyu.

"Jesus bloody Christ."

"Shh," I venture. He twists his neck to look at me.

The litany varies in the morning when the doctors come. They are as unpalatable as the Son of God.

"Pigs!" shouts Don. "You doctors know nothing. Get your hands off me. Pig."

In fifty years of practice amongst brain changes of every type, including frontal lobe damage and disinhibition, Dr Ferguson has been called a bear but never a pig. He stops in his tracks, flushed and stupefied.

The wife beseeches him to tranquillise the patient, but the doctors prefer to hand him over to the psychologist to "help him make peace with his condition."

"You're also a pig," flashes Don at the psychologist.

The other elderly patient has travelled down from further north on the continent where no rehab hospitals exist. Four similar sons in colourful robes accompany him. His name is Malik.

"Allahu Akbar," they murmur together at regular intervals.

"Jesus Christ," interjects Donald, starting a call-and-response that will go on for days.

Matron is getting desperate because Malik won't eat. The sons stand over his tray, sniffing the food like a king's poison-testers.

In a moment of rare cross-cultural insight, Dr Fabrizio says, "Ask the Jewish girl what he can eat, kosher and halaal are the same."

Matron comes over to me with a menu card and we work through it together, circumventing the ham.

"Jesus Christ!" from Don. The sons stare across the beds at him and draw their curtains close.

One night, Don's wife folds tearfully in on herself as the chorus increases in vehemence. Looking at her, I see she is more wretched from heresy than hospital.

"Allahu Akbar," comes from across the ward, and a grinding of teeth from my side of the headboard.

Malik is walking within a fortnight and the sons take him home.

Don eventually wears himself out and withdraws into a quiet self-loathing.

Noluthando

SHE IS ELEVEN years old, a survivor of the roads. The hospital does not yet have a dedicated children's ward so she is put in with us. Even the sickest adults try to promise her a future and save the best morsels off their plates for her.

She is my neighbour on the ward. There's less than a metre between our beds. She has never been this close to a white woman before. Sometimes she bravely chats to herself or hums. I love to hear the steady, even rhythm of her breathing on a good night. It reminds me of my own children.

Noluthando is intensely interested in my visitors and appraises each one with an unabashed stare, eager for them to leave so we can share the treats they brought. She packs and unpacks my toiletries from the bedside cupboard as often as I'll let her, sniffing each bottle as if for the first time. She's an ordinary but hurt little girl in an extraordinary place.

When, after several months, she stands up out of her small wheelchair and hobbles into the ward on a walking frame, a loud cheer goes up. She grins like a triathlon *victrix*, generous in her feat.

She parks the walking frame between our beds with a proprietorial air.

One morning, after she's cleaned her neck and face as thoroughly as a kitten, we hear her whimpering. "Come somebody. There's blood on my panty."

The women in the ward change gear into a primal unity. I lean across to soothe her but I cannot reach her. Her nurse draws the curtains, and we hear, "Don't worry sweetie, you're not sick, you're just becoming a woman."

"No. I don't want it," Noluthando moans in perplexity.

Her remaining family, all male, give her a small fluffy toy, which she holds to her cheek in order to sleep.

This is the place where children grow up too quickly and too slowly.

Picnic

MY FRIEND LAYS on a picnic in the early moments of the new century in the grounds of the cement rehab hospital.

We are both sickened by the weeks and months of hospital food, its brown smells and sorry vegetables. I, the transmogrified, am wheeled to temporary freedom while she swings the basket alongside.

Within the army of workers who keep the big edifice functioning, there is a sub-army of tactful, clever gardeners. It is autumn and cold, and the stretches of blanched grass are surrounded by beds of spiky indigenous plants as hardy as their context. There are splashes of improbable colour and an occasional wave of moisture from the spray.

We sit in a loving patch of sun, and begin to unpack the meal. The basket is padded inside with classic gingham and produces surprises from each small compartment. Wine glasses…shiny cutlery.

We eat salty crisp things with mediterranean dips. Fresh salad. Gooseberries. The joy of the world re-enters me on my tongue. It's been so long, yet it's so easy to identify the tastes.

"Another drink?" says the picnic virtuoso, relaxing into her warm coat.

Looking up at the hospital, I see hundreds of windows, with some dim internal silhouettes. No open windows at all. From the garden my ward looks quiet and ordered. It doesn't feel like that at all when I'm inside. The change in perspective is refreshing.

We start to pack away, dribbling the last of our drinks on to the lawn. The basket is shut again, and we toil back up the path knowing that the day will have to go on among a hundred sick others, and their carers.

I can still taste the chickpeas and tomatoes, and feel the reassuring imprint of her hug as we re-enter.

Cluster Three

Adaptation

Buoyant

WE DISCUSS GRAVITY. A young paraplegic says he can't feel the earth under him any longer. How can we all feel so leaden and so weightless at the same time? How can the something and the nothing of a substance look the same?

Running up stairs is a half-forgotten melody strained after; embracing the beloved with two arms, a phantom vision.

We gaze at each other, phalanx on wheels, and marvel at our own group solidity.

Inside hydrotherapy, it is as foggy and humid as a terrarium. We have the grace of mermaids, once lowered into the water.

Limbs hooked and heavy on land shimmer above gravity. There are six of us in the pool with a therapist as smooth as a dolphin and tireless of concentration. She stretches us, makes benign resistance, holds the centre under a choppy surface.

No desolation can survive this glorious buoyancy.

Homecoming

EMIGRATED SIBLINGS AND friends say the journey from the airport into the city on return trips is weirdly familiar yet unfamiliar at the same time. Home is as old as one's skin but as elusive as an object seen through the wrong end of a telescope.

Coming home from a rehab hospital after five months is similar. The house is full of familiar landmarks and a cheery "Welcome home Mom!" banner, but everything has changed. Obstacles spring up where there were none before. I contemplate my winter dressing gown on its old hook behind the door at a height I can no longer reach myself. I'm confronted by the new Karen in various mirrors. There were none in hospital. I wonder if I'd feel safer back there.

On the first morning back I wake to fresh garden smells and, at last, the taste of proper coffee. I hear my children chatting over breakfast, a forgetful moment of simple normalcy. My spirits sing.

Home, yes, home.

A few months later, a large orphaned puppy comes into the family. He establishes the eccentric habit of sitting on a kitchen chair. I ponder this audacity. One day I wheel past him and I realize we're at eye level. He offers me a paw. I shake it. When I stand up or walk around he jumps off his perch. He only sits on his chair when I'm in mine.

He's just making a special effort to accommodate to me at my own level.

Hemispheres

THREE HUNDRED HIGH-SCHOOL English teachers are assembled in an auditorium for staff training. I'm seated in a chair on a podium in front of them, my first foray back into the working world since the big time-out.

I'm to teach Shakespearean comedy, itself rich in the incongruities of a varied humanity. It starts well. I'm lecturing confidently, as of old, at home in my subject matter. I gather momentum, enjoying the great playwright's splashing of carnivalesque mishap on to the bigger life-affirming canvas of comedy. I'm feeling pretty affirmed myself, a professional again in my own domain.

But a sensation of a new kind is rising in me, a bass hum beneath the melody. Something palpable but impalpable is wrong with my relationship with the class. I can't tell whether it's a lack or a blockage of some kind. Or both. This has never happened before.

"Excuse me for a moment, please," I say.

The teachers are watching me quizzically but sympathetically, murmuring amongst themselves. I feel naked.

The pause secures me the clarity to locate the problem. I have unconsciously been teaching to only one half of the auditorium. The other half has vanished into my alienated left spatial field. I snatch a glance at the room, half-expecting to see a barricade down the middle, corresponding with the two hemispheres of my brain. Many people have heard of the man who mistook his wife for a hat[1]. It seems as if I'm the woman who mistook her left side for a vacuum.

So this is what my therapists mean by 'compensation'. I manoeuvre my chair from its slightly diagonal position to face the teachers frontally, and the missing half swings back into my compass. I pick up the reins of my thought, grinning like a character from the sub-plot.

The weirdest thing about a stroke is that you lose things you didn't know you had. The faculty that eludes me in the lecture is called 'proprioception', meaning 'one's own' perception. It's the internal self-regulation system that gives feedback on the relative status of the body's parts.

It will be many months before I stop scraping the left-hand wall of the passage or leaving the hot tap dripping.

Luckily this is comedy and not tragedy.

---

1   Oliver Sacks *The Man Who Mistook His Wife For A Hat And Other Clinical Tales.* (1985: Summit Books)

Intersection

I HAVE TO take my driving test again at the age of forty. I'm delighted to get my licence, and am besotted with my sleek adapted car, its nifty steering-wheel spinner and resting pedal for the paralysed foot.

But my co-ordination isn't what it was. And Joburg is still Joburg.

On the way back from school one morning, I turn right at a huge intersection across four lanes of traffic. I'm enjoying the old normalcy.

I make it across but an extra two lanes yield into mine.

Suddenly I'm at the blaring confluence of multiple lanes. A bully of a taxi roars in on my right side. At exactly that moment, another taxi charges up on the inside lane.

For a second, my internal map disintegrates. I cannot hold the stimuli coming in from two sides simultaneously. The epicentre of my focus dissolves. A sense of vertigo takes over and I fall through the net of my own reflexes.

I swerve, missing another car by two inches. A sickening intimation of the crunch of metal-upon-metal washes over me. But it's okay.

That's the last time I get behind the wheel for a long time.

Slapstick

ERRORS HAVE BECOME more dangerous but no less ridiculous than they were before.

Lift doors close like a vice on shoulders reversing too slowly. The city is an alien new geometry of precarious access.

The long way round is invariably the safe way round.

Not accepting help is futile.

Heart skips a beat and bruises slow to heal show up on unreachable patches of body.

Small mahogany tables had better stay out the way.

There's no sabbatical from clumsiness.

But if we don't laugh, we cry.

Rest Room

WE VEER OFF the hot tarmac into a vast complex of consecutive refuellings. Shell Ultra City. The petrol attendants cheerfully fill up and scrape insect matter off the windscreen.

Whole families disgorge into the fast-food places whose only virtue is coolth. The rancid eggs swim across the plates.

A humane planner has provided safe shelter for the truck drivers of the all-night routes. Here, there is no risk of the metallic maiming which will send them to the rehabilitation hospital in Johannesburg. The drivers hail each other at high volume:

"To Kimberley, you?"

"Moçambique."

"Go well."

Under the lone tree there is a climbing frame for the car-cramped limbs to stretch and swing. Rural and city children scrutinise each other's shoes and clothes. Their skin broils until the parents chivvy them back to the car, with packets-full of more food to meet their boredom on the highway at the other end of the crescent.

I hobble off to the rest rooms on my stick. I follow the signs but they are not propitious. 'Disabled Toilet'. One does prefer one's toilet to be Abled.

Coming back I see the same semantics – 'Disabled Parking'. That's the one that hosts a large vehicle full of healthy people, too avid for the oily eggs to find another bay.

If I didn't need my crutch to stay upright, I would be brandishing it at them.

Sardine Run

My son and daughter, sensible of their mother's favourite activities slipping away, are determined to get me into the sea.

I'm wheeled into the ocean in my chair until I'm hip-high in the water, flanked by two exuberant children. It's a beautiful day.

All is well and the bracing taste of salt overcomes the taste of shame in my mouth. It's sardine season and we see slivers of silver all around. I feel their cold little fish-bodies dancing around mine. A few nibble at my static flesh but it's not unpleasant. Until I notice a solid sensation under my buttocks. My chair has sunk its wheels all the way into the hungry sand, seat hugging the sea floor. This is not going to be an easy retraction. I'm waist-high in the water and getting panicky, but I giggle for appearance's sake. Could this ingenuous experiment have been pure folly?

Small Julia is hopping from foot to foot, dark eyes averted. Driven by necessity, her brother goes up to a group of burly fathers lounging on the sand with cooler bags open. A toddler rubs sand vigorously into one man's chest hair.

"Hi, I'm Raphael, could you please come and help me get my mom out the sea?"

He gestures at the back of my sunken chair and the circle of transfixed but helpless onlookers, mainly mothers and children.

A caravan of fathers give six big heaves and I catapult backwards, drenched and liberated.

Back at the hotel, the manager asks the children to hose me down on the lawn, wheels and all. He says,

"So you had that swim you wanted, Miss. Where there's a will there's a way."

A sardine whooshes out from the spokes of the wheel.

Trip to the Tate

ON A VISIT to London, my brothers Alan and Michael bundle my wheelchair and me into the car and we set off for the new Tate Modern. We are buffeted across the bridge over a churning Thames.

When we enter the gallery, a line of empty wheelchairs welcomes us. Al cheerfully wheels me along in mine, through gracious rooms and interesting exhibits. When I need the bathroom, I find it accommodating and spotless. However, when I reach for the grab rail, it comes out of the wall.

A couple of hours and two storeys later, the same thing happens. There I am, wavering around on one leg, a Picasso on the other side of the wall and a chrome bar in my hand.

This time Mike, indignant of imperfection, reports the design fault to management.

Forty-eight hours later I answer the phone.

"Ms Lazar?"

"Speaking."

"We're calling to tell you that your toilet at the Tate is ready, madam."

Sink Or Swim

TEN-THIRTY IN THE morning. My mother-in-law and I are sitting in drenching rain in an open stadium with the floodlights on. For the most improbable occasion, a gala. Well-trained paediatric athletes from all over the country are assembled around the high-tech heated pool, whilst the officials debate cancellation but continue in the interests of bureaucratic face-saving.

The agency that brings us here is the Central Gauteng Aquatics. This time our landlocked province is host. Our new black swimmers queue tolerantly for their mispronounced names.

The children dive flawlessly off their plinths, one to each lane. Their speed and grace are dazzling, but visibility is poor.

I'm in my wheelchair, half under an awning with a plastic cover over my legs. I screech keenly for my child, he of the red cap speeding backwards in the ninth lane. Until a team-mate comes up behind me and says,

"That's not Raph."

I'm embarrassed but that physique is common around here. A parent from the adjacent team moves close to the edge and yells for two identical girls, not her own, dimly appearing in the water.

"Go twin," making projectile movements at the disappearing limbs. And then, for fairness, "Go other twin!"

I do a mental head-count of children heading for pneumonia, but they just keep on coming back for more and more heats. Heats? My thermos of tea brings envious glances.

The mood is further darkened by the sight of long lines of children in hooded capes, Klan-style, filing around in team colours. My child pops up in front of me, snug in his fur-lined crimson robe, eyes blue as the water and undeterred by wet upon wet.

Someone is making pancakes in a van. They go down faster than they're cooked. The hunger of a thousand cold active children is bigger even than the ludicrousness of the event.

As if the downpour weren't enough, teenage rave music is thundering over the public address system. Someone dedicates a roar to an unfortunate girl having her birthday submerged. Our boy hangs his dripping towels over the back of the wheelchair in exchange for dry ones. I feel vaguely useful.

I numbly wonder if there is a Peripheral Gauteng Aquatics and what the weather is like there. Eventually, I need to be pushed back to the entrance, but the ramps are clogged. Dozens of children are nestled in sleeping bags on the paths, desperate for warmth and rest. They pull terrible faces at the lady on muddy wheels who

necessitates their moving aside. Nobody wants to **budge**.
This is not a good moment for courtesy.

Back home, the vapour rises from us. And,

"Thanks for your commitment, Ma."

Waterworld

JULES TURNS TEN at the end of summer. We go with a small team of girls to Waterworld on the East Rand. This area once hosted active goldmines that still shoot their scaffolds and yellow waste piles high over flat settlements.

And here, off the highway and into this arid terrain, we enter Waterworld. I am wheeled along lightly in my wheelchair by a friend, on paved paths that I share with prams and skateboards. The architects have spared nothing on this conspicuous blue fantasy. Chutes descend from watery heights at all compass points. Children coast down shrilly on their tummies or bob about in bloated orange tyres. We watch in hot amazement.

Picnickers braai meat in abundance and face their roasting red backs to the sun. Even the babies are blotchy from sunburn and overeating. Some small township children at the edge of the water obviously cannot swim, but there are neither life jackets nor lifeguards included in the entrance ticket to wondrous Waterworld.

We find a picnic spot, then chaperone the timid girls through their first slither. And the sea! A huge expanse of water breaking rhythmically without the moon.

Then the noise begins. We are so close to the major international airport that land is cheap here, though silence unaffordable. An Air Cameroon plane swoops low over the ocean. Our girls block their noses and duck under the water to avoid its rattling nether wheels. Then a bright green plane enters our airspace, member of a cheap dotcom airline company. It elicits a collective scream from the sea, "Big Green Machine!"

Loudspeakers in our palm trees blare rock and sakkie sakkie songs. The Boeings keep descending. Our teenage boys walk stiffly to save dignity in their waterlogged baggies, alternately skulking and preening. The girls straggle back and forth with hair wet and rat-tailed. Jules keeps trying her favourite slides with friends charging good-humouredly behind. Air Canada keeps a decorous vertical distance.

The bathroom for disabled people is in a slippery ersatz cave with handy stalagmites for grabbing. I feel like a challenged early hominid in here.

Finally, water-satiated, the children spy an airborne pleasure that isn't swooping, but rotating – 'Ferris-wheel!' – and so we traipse and wheel back to the dry parking lot for one last tacky treat.

We take them home for an early night, for tomorrow is school.

The Hope School

IT OCCUPIES BEAUTIFUL sprawling cottages, all tawny stone and bright wisteria. Its neighbour is a shameless pink hotel extruding from the ridge.

When the bell rings, a community of high-school students pours out of the classrooms. The ones who can walk push the wheelchairs of those who can't. Every imaginable type of body and face attends here.

I watch a pair of youngsters entwine hands shyly. A circle of girls passes earphones from person to person. They croon in unison. Others concentrate on the dexterity required for non-stop text messaging.

"They seem like regular teenagers," I comment to the teacher on duty.

"No, not really," he says. "That one has AIDS, that one has autism, that one has cerebral palsy, that one…God knows what."

I move away from him; maybe one needs to become hard here. I'm here for a teaching practical, so I drive to the pre-primary school to observe my student. The setting is colourful and access is fluent. The little children are intrigued to see a disabled adult and enchanted by the fire engine red of my scooter.

"You're a good role model," says the teacher, offering me a misshapen jam sandwich.

A child with ornate braids bounces up to me on plump legs. "Hey ma'am, I'm Lerato, it's my number five birthday today, so can I push your hooter?"

"It was her birthday last week too," smiles the teacher drily.

Before I know it, a line of twenty small children is growing behind me to follow Lerato's cue. One by one they come forward to toot the shrill electronic button.

Finally only one child is left. "Your turn Sandile," says the teacher.

He has only a torso. No legs and arms. He's lying flat on his stomach on a low black plastic scooter. He manoeuvres his way forward with surprising twists and propulsions. He looks up at me with bright expectant eyes. I wonder what to do.

Sandile wriggles himself on his scooter up closer towards my bigger scooter, lifts his exquisite little face towards the dashboard. I hear the familiar beep and find Sandile's chin on the hooter, pushing the button purposefully. He rumbles off to class amidst infirm children being wheeled into lessons in hospital beds.

I look up to find my student crying.

Encounter

IT IS A college, airy, with splashes of foliage amidst apartheid architecture. The avid young lope around with lowslung jeans and backpacks, sharing crisps and sandwiches. A thousand text messages flicker back and forth. Girls dive for a rugby ball with boys on the lawn between clusters of friends studying together.

The scarlet scooter purrs along the concrete walkway, front basket brimming with books. Three young men approach me with sweet curiosity. They are all muscular and slender, in sleeveless vests and baggy pants. One wears silver laces in his Converse takkies and beaded dreadlocks in a ponytail. The one who speaks has kind, intelligent eyes behind tortoise-shell spectacle frames.

"Ma'am, who are you, which department? We see you each and every day. You are a character."

But, in class, the scooter is just part of the furniture and my students are used to me.

Luleka

LULEKA IS A tall man, solidly built, bearded around a soft smile. He has been blind since birth. An expert cane takes him round campus. I have seldom seen such absolute focus. My courage rallies every time I see his.

He thanks me often for my mentorship, but challenges my superfluous apologies. He asks me to describe myself during the briefing session.

"I'm medium-sized, as high as your shoulder. I have short hair. I drive a scooter because the left side of my body doesn't work so well."

This is a man with little self-pity.

He has raised money to go to Paterson College in the USA for his teaching practical. He goes with another student who can only see silhouettes. He has flown before, though not for thirty hours. She has not. He guides them both, with a light touch of her elbow. Her name is Cheryl and she is shy but fashionable. She wears leggings and baggy shirts and ankle boots.

They come back ebullient from their brave new horizons. Luleka regales me with tales of courteous assistants in stores as big as hangars. He describes technology so advanced he can teach with three senses. He has felt Braille beneath his feet at the corners by traffic lights. He has acquired an expanded curriculum that teaches deaf-blind children about hygiene, money, autonomy.

At the end of the debriefing, he hands me their gift – a comfortable T-shirt with BOSTON emblazoned in red.

"Is it blue?" Luleka wants to know. "I asked for navy-blue."

He's come from so little but he shares so much. Especially his vision.

Interface

I'M WITH THE neurologist. He's boyish and scholarly and loves the sleuth work of his discipline.

I ask him if he can explain why my second language has gone AWOL.

"Yes…" he answers brightly, "or at least maybe. Some research suggests that prosody is stored on the right hemisphere of the brain. That's in your affected half."

"Prosody?" It's an old-fashioned term used to teach poetry in an old-fashioned way. Poetry is my field. Science is his. Yet here they are, met. I'm intrigued.

"Yes, we believe the right hemisphere may govern the brain's grasp of pitch, cadence and rhythm."

A vision arises of musical quavers, crotchets and beats swarming round my head.

"I've had stroke patients coming round with a broad Scottish accent from out of the blue," says sleuth-doctor.

"So how do you suggest I get my French back?"

"Try reading French poetry."

We smile.

Acknowledgements

SPECIAL THANKS TO:

Colleen Higgs and Modjadji Books for bringing this
    writing to light;

Nella Freund for her scrupulous and subtle editing;

My brilliant team of physical and spiritual therapists for
    showing me the way;

All my wonderful friends and colleagues for encouraging
    me to write, thrive, and grow strong;

Ashleigh Harris for her steady, loving presence in the
    toughest early days;

Mbali Mabanga for her strength, patience and
    compassion;

Matthew Chaskalson and Susan Levy for their loyalty
    and generosity;

Stan, Claire, Gillian, John and Alan Lazar and their
    families for their unconditional love and support;

Raphael and Julia Chaskalson for their love and courage
    and capaciousness, and for being able to laugh, at me,
    and with me.

Isabel Hofmeyr on Hemispheres:

" A stroke on one hemisphere of the brain crosses over to manifest ... on the opposite side of the body".

What does it mean to find oneself suddenly living at this lethal crossing?

This exquisite book illuminates how to live with and beyond loss.

A superb filigree of acute and finely-crafted pieces, *Hemispheres* narrates the journey of re-composing life, joy and love from the 'foreign citadel' of a body made alien through stroke.

Wry, ironic, comic, joyous, desolate, celebratory, surreal, this mosaic of feeling reconfigures love from loss; each subtle fragment a tessera against time.

As the pieces delve deep into the self, they reach beyond it. The rehabilitation hospital reeks of personal loss even as it becomes a microcosm of contemporary South Africa. Broken bodies deformed by carnage and violence accumulate in the ward. The medical hierarchy enacts deep-seated forms of South African authoritarianism, the losses of the past inflicted and self-inflicted in petty and cruel ways.

The book becomes a quiet odyssey of affirming life in the face of death. The pieces themselves, weightless and profound, light and dark, half and whole, mirror the contradictions of wrenching life from loss. "

Isabel Hofmeyr, Professor of African Literature,
University of the Witwatersrand

CONTEMPORARY MEMOIR TITLES BY MODJAJI

Invisible Earthquake:
A Women's Journal Through Stillbirth
by Malika Ndlovu

Undisciplined Heart
by Jane Katjavivi

Reclaiming the L-word:
Sappho's Daughters Out in Africa
edited by Alleyn Diesel

http://modjaji.book.co.za